This house and its every room.

Chloe Clinton

BookLeaf Publishing

Presentation by *BookLeaf Publishing*

Web: www.bookleafpub.com

E-mail: info@bookleafpub.com

ISBN: 9789395890755

First edition 2023

This collection is dedicated to my younger self - the dedication is extended to anyone who helped her.

ACKNOWLEDGEMENT

I would like to acknowledge the Kaurna, Turrbal, and Jagera people who are the Traditional Custodians of the land that I live, work and write on. I would also like to pay respect to the Elders both past and present of the Adelaide Plains, Meanjin land, and the surrounding Queensland area.

PREFACE

Writing as a form of expression comes with many challenges and in the writing of this collection, I have come across many doubtful thoughts - "Will people want to read what I write?", "How will I write something people want to read?", "What if I have shared too much of myself?" and so on. In publishing this book it will be one more step forward in knowing that I write for myself, this is my experience, and if somebody reads it, it's because they will have wanted to. My collection is aimed at those who appreciate the written word as an outlet and those who would like to read a piece of me.

A Glass House.

Please do not touch me.
For you are fragile.
I am the stone,
being thrown in the glass house that is you.
I am reckless,
thrown around careless and aimlessly
and I will make you fall to pieces.

I was a glass house,
until I came crashing down.
Now I am the rubble - still as fragile,
as the glass house, I once used to be
and, as the rubble laying beneath the debris

I do not want to see you become me.

Nothing at all.

Half of me wants to lay in bed;
watch the sunset,
do nothing.
The other parts of me want to; cut off my own
head,
watch some T.V. -
do everything.

Pieces yet to be lost.

Teeth falling to the bottom of my mouth
with my jaw unhinged.
Blood begins to fill the corners of the couch.
What's left of your dignity has now flooded my
carpets.
Dust covers all of the surfaces in my apartment.
You have not left my bed
because you will not leave the depths of my
head -
you'll stay here a little longer.
My teeth falling out one by one,
I'll start a collection;
the pieces that I have lost of myself, what I
could have become.

The pieces I have lost and the pieces I am yet to
lose.

Bathroom floor.

After the third hour of being a prisoner to my
own bathroom floor,
I didn't feel like mine anymore...

How many pills until I am no longer real?

Cold.

Both pink tiles
and fairy lights,
make the night seem less cold -
even though I have spent all of this time alone.

I sit in the mess I have made of myself
and loathe every part of me that used to exist.
It is in the bathtub, that I sit.
Cold.

The blanket fort I have made.

I try to hide.
In the corners, under covers.
If only I could let you,
let you inside.

Some room for you…

To have a room and somebody in it.
To have a room and to let you in,
to have the space to let you listen.
To have a room is one thing. To have you in it is
another.

I'm picking at the wall again.

I'll fix myself later -
just like the hole in the wall.
You put it there, when someone asks we say you
fell.
You put a hole in the wall
and like we said, I'll fix it later.

Chores.

Just like a chore.
I am forced to love you,
because if I do not, then how will the house stay
clean?
Just like a chore.
You are ingrained into my mind's forefront.
Thinking about you all day
but then when it comes to:
I will be reluctant,
I will feel disgusting.
Removing your hair from the drain,
bleaching the grout that holds the stains.
Waiting for next week -
just like a chore.

Cup of tea

I've been not just losing my mind but losing
sleep.
I woke 72 times last night and at 4.37 pm I woke
for the 73rd time.
I contemplated whether the steps from my door
to the bathroom would be too many, whether on
the 3rd, 4th, or 7th I would watch the walls spin
around me and I would become tied to the cold
beige tiles beneath.
I turn my body to face the curtains that are
merely just a length of fabric hanging between
the sunlight and me; my body has been so
desperately pleading for.

My feet hover over the carpet begging to feel
something other than the navy blue sheets
they've been tangled between for nights and
days on end.
Begging to feel the weight of my body.

Walking. Counting. Breathing.

I step closer to the bathroom to try and at least
grip onto the walls - stay upright.

Today Tom, today is a day which I am begging
for a cup of tea, to be exact, 73.
To keep me here
To keep me intact.

Wanted.

To be looked at like I was wanted again,
even just for the night.
Laying on your bed -
curtains closed but there's still light.
To lie down with your hands on my thighs.
To be in your room,
one more time.

I am decaying.

Have I ever told you,
that I fall apart at the end of every day?
As soon as I walk out the doors -
one step in front of the other.
I slowly crumble until I get to my doorstep.
Losing bits of me along the way.
Then I get home, lay down, and decay -
until I wake up and do it all again.
Picking up the pieces of me from yesterday,
to watch it all fall away once more.

This is the Garden.

Last night,
I buried my body in the front yard -
Beneath the flowers in the garden.
I lay in silence as they dig their way into my
skin, burrowing their roots into my veins -
Until I am intertwined with the floral display
that faces outwards onto the pathway that I used
to pace.

Seams.

I've been pulling apart the seams of my favorite
bedsheets.
Just to feel productive.
So that I'm not just laying waiting to wake up,
instead, I am being destructive.
Pulling the seams of the sheets until there is no
longer any warmth left for me.

Gas.

The gas in my apartment started to leak, I leaned
out of my window at 3 am, all so I could breathe
easy.
I sat there for hours so that it didn't eat me
whole, so I wouldn't get devoured by the gas
pipe that hadn't even sprung a leak.
I wish I just fell asleep. Look what you've done
to me.

Taking the Bins in.

I know I am a disappointment because even on
my worst days,
I won't remember to bring the bins in.
So they'll rest out on the curb a little while
longer while I walk into unit number 2;
Thinking about how I am my own stranger.

I wish I could say it was you who kept me afloat
But you are different now,
You have changed.
I wish I could say it was you I needed the most
on these bad days but somehow,
Things will always, yet never stay the same.

So I stay unable to bring the bins in.

Mess you made.

It's day 3 of you not here with me
and I'm still stuck -
clinging to the mess you made.
Your clothes, my floor,
your white oversized tee draped over the handle
of my door, your charger plugged into my wall.
The smell of you is stuck in my green bedsheets,
and I can't bring myself to wash them.
so I'll sleep on my carpets.

Today was a Friday.

Yesterday was a Thursday. I know this because today is a Friday and tomorrow will be Saturday. Time is something that's never been good to me. when I was 7 I fell and scraped both knees, then screaming through the blood pooling through the cuts on my hands - Mum sat me down to say, "You're okay, give it time, you will get better". Just like that, 2 weeks went by, and sure enough, what were then wounds that plastered my skin became flakey and soon to shed. Then when I turned 9, I lost a friend, and again, with time things began to feel alright. the photos of her kept me company while the whole world slept, but not me. Too scared to close my eyes and see her when I woke. Too scared to fall asleep and choke on the memory of her patting a seat beside her for me to sit. 11 came around and I cried on my birthday because I felt like nobody loved me - again for the 12th, 13th, 14th, and so on. Fast-forward to 17 and I felt a loss of self. The greatest loss, the build-up like a storm, clouds slowly covering the sun, the final straw. The rain clouds began to pour. Now 20 I'm still watching the dust collect on the shelf of my apartment.

Mum would have cleaned them by now - but I'm
not her, and I never will be.

God is watching me.

God can see what I do in your room.
God can see all that is said to be a sin, all that is
unholy.
God is listening -
and he won't stop. It's like a running
commentary of my life and it won't shut the fuck
up.
God, I am sorry but not for what I've done.
I am the result of your mistakes, the decisions
you made were wrong.
because God if you are so holy, why have you
punished me? Why is this what you want?
God, I am tired and sleep-deprived. I've been
miswired.
God this was you, God if you want me in heaven
you'll need to re-invent me, wipe my past clean,
make me brand new.
All that you have seen of me - my naked body,
dirty sheets - all of me, unholy. Bitter. Sweet.
Unholy.

I am bleeding too.

In the same way you bleed, I bleed too. Except when I bleed, the blood is for you. I want you to hold me. Cradle me now. Tell me that I haven't let you down.

I know there have been many promises and none yet to be kept. But let me say that when I come home and lay in bed, I feel forever in your debt. I wish I could save you. Darling baby, sweet little thing, I promise that one day you will feel complete.

I'm watching from my bedroom, the television that sits on top of a cardboard box, thinking how lucky we are to have made it. The aerial antenna is in pieces and the 10 pm program glitches. I am happy to have broken our promise and I am glad to have felt this. If you could be here, sitting next to me, I would tell you that this is all i've needed to be happy.

For a long time I was longing, yearning for a company as sweet as yours. I would tell you that you're okay, that I will take all of your flaws. "Darling baby, sweet gentle angel, you are pure and fragile, I won't let anybody hurt you," I say from the mattress on the floor in the bedroom as we watch the television propped up on top of a cardboard box with an antenna in half.

Surrounded by white brick walls I spend my first night alone in my apartment wishing you could see this. Although soon enough the feeling will wear off. Months pass by and I listen to the sound of the wind shaking my screen door, I'm sitting in the bathroom, I don't want to be here anymore. I am sorry, I let you down, i'm sorry for today. This week has been a long one, all I have felt is pain. How many pills until I am not real anymore? I'm sitting and sinking into

The cold pink tiles - staring into the toilet wondering if I have the courage to stand up and walk myself back to bed. I needed you then, why weren't you there? Little darling girl, sweet beautiful thing, this is not your responsibility. No one ever told you that, so watch the words fall from my mouth as I collapse.
You remember driving through the hills, Dad in the driver's seat, Mum right beside? Your sister sitting next to us, we close our eyes. He's been speeding for quite some time, Mum needs you to sing, "A, B, C, D -". We swerve another corner. Shaking in the backseat singing to make sure

nobody feels the heat. Baby darling, sweet little thing, that was not your responsibility.

You're in a constant panic as of late. No one meant it when they said everything would be okay. So now you're feeling like your fingertips are going to break. All there is to do is sit alone, cry in your room. Slowly wither away as the darkness consumes you…

In the same way I bleed, you have bled too. It's just that I am bleeding dry and it has now come time to turn off the T.V. and sit in my own silence. You want me to hold you, I want to be able to. Cradle you now and to tell you that I haven't let us down.

This house and its every room.

This house and its every room.
It has seen so many things of me to be very true.
I have ached. I have promised.
I have laid down my heavy heart on the carpets -
the floor of my living room and let it bleed dry.
I have spilled my every secret and my very guts
into the dirt-packed spaces between the yellow
linoleum tiles on the kitchen floor - overflowing
and in waves - rolling underneath the oven.
Where many things hide.
Dead moths, half-cooked spiral pasta that fell
down the gap where the bench should meet the
oven side - that was about 3 months and 9 days
ago now. Tears of mine and maybe some of
yours too.
The painted white brick walls have seen me at
my rock bottom.
Kneeling down desperate for air. Begging to
breathe. Pleading to know that it's not just me.
I wonder if they know how hard this life has
been, or maybe it's been worse than they have
seen.
I wonder if the toilet has been cleaned since I've
gone or whether there is still the residue sitting

sunk to the bottom from the 40 or maybe the
50-odd pills I flushed that I used to hoard for
safekeeping (just in case things got too hard
again), in case my thumbs, like as though they
will fracture in the wind.
Maybe I didn't want to be screaming for air
anymore, just in case, I didn't know how I got
here, didn't know where I was anymore.

My bedroom, it has held all of the clothes that
no longer stretch over my body the way they did
before, the ones from even before that, that now
hang from my stronger shoulders.
The fabric is merely a barrier between the
intimacy of self, the damaged skin being hidden
away from the damaged world.

Every room of this house,
has let me down.
One day I will not be able to recall - the feeling
of sinking into my bathroom floor beside the
pipe work in the corner, wedged between the
pink tiles grouted white, in complete agony.
I will instead rewind and reminisce on photos of
a white ceramic bowl with a sink direct in front,
pink tiled walls surrounding what was once a
cage that kept me safe, and now a photo of a
bathroom that I used to sing in.